AF599115

BELLWETHER MEDIA · MINNEAPOLIS, MN

Torque brims with excitement perfect for thrill-seekers of all kinds. Discover daring survival skills, explore uncharted worlds, and marvel at mighty engines and extreme sports. In *Torque* books, anything can happen. Are you ready?

This edition first published in 2025 by Bellwether Media, Inc.

Library of Congress Cataloging-in-Publication Data

Names: Adamson, Thomas K., 1970- author.
Title: Nikola Jokić / by Thomas K. Adamson.
Description: Minneapolis MN : Bellwether Media, 2025. | Series: Torque Sports superstars | Includes bibliographical references and index. | Audience: Ages 7-12 | Audience: Grades 4-6 | Summary: "Engaging images accompany information about Nikola Jokić. The combination of high-interest subject matter and light text is intended for students in grades 3 through 7"– Provided by publisher.
Identifiers: LCCN 2024010421 (print) | LCCN 2024010422 (ebook) | ISBN 9798893040371 (library binding) | ISBN 9781644879771 (ebook)
Subjects: LCSH: Jokić, Nikola, 1995–Juvenile literature. | Basketball players–Serbia–Biography–Juvenile literature. | Basketball players–United States–Biography–Juvenile literature.
Classification: LCC GV884.J65 A73 2024 (print) | LCC GV884.J65 (ebook) | DDC 796.323092 [B]–dc23/eng/20240307
LC record available at https://lccn.loc.gov/2024010421
LC ebook record available at https://lccn.loc.gov/2024010422

Editor: Kieran Downs   Designer: Gabriel Hilger

Printed in the United States of America, North Mankato, MN.

TABLE OF CONTENTS

BIG FINALS WIN

It is Game 5 of the 2023 **Finals**. The Nuggets face the Heat. A little more than two minutes remain. The Nuggets trail by one point.

Nuggets player Nikola Jokić gets the ball. He turns and drives to the hoop. He reaches for the basket and scores. The Nuggets take the lead! The Nuggets go on to win their first Finals **championship**.

Jokić's Big Game

Jokić scored 28 points in Game 5!

WHO IS NIKOLA JOKIĆ?

Nikola Jokić is a **center** in the **National Basketball Association** (NBA). Jokić is a great passer and shooter. Other teams find it hard to stop him.

JOKER

Fans call Jokić "The Joker."

NIKOLA JOKIĆ

BIRTHDAY	February 19, 1995
HOMETOWN	Sombor, Serbia
POSITION	center
HEIGHT	6 feet 11 inches
DRAFTED	Denver Nuggets in the 2nd round (41st overall) of the 2014 NBA Draft

Jokić won the NBA **Most Valuable Player** (MVP) award in two straight seasons. He led the Denver Nuggets to the team's first-ever NBA Finals in 2023.

A STAR IN SERBIA

Jokić was born in Sombor, Serbia. During his childhood, the country was at war. The Jokić family was often left without electricity for weeks.

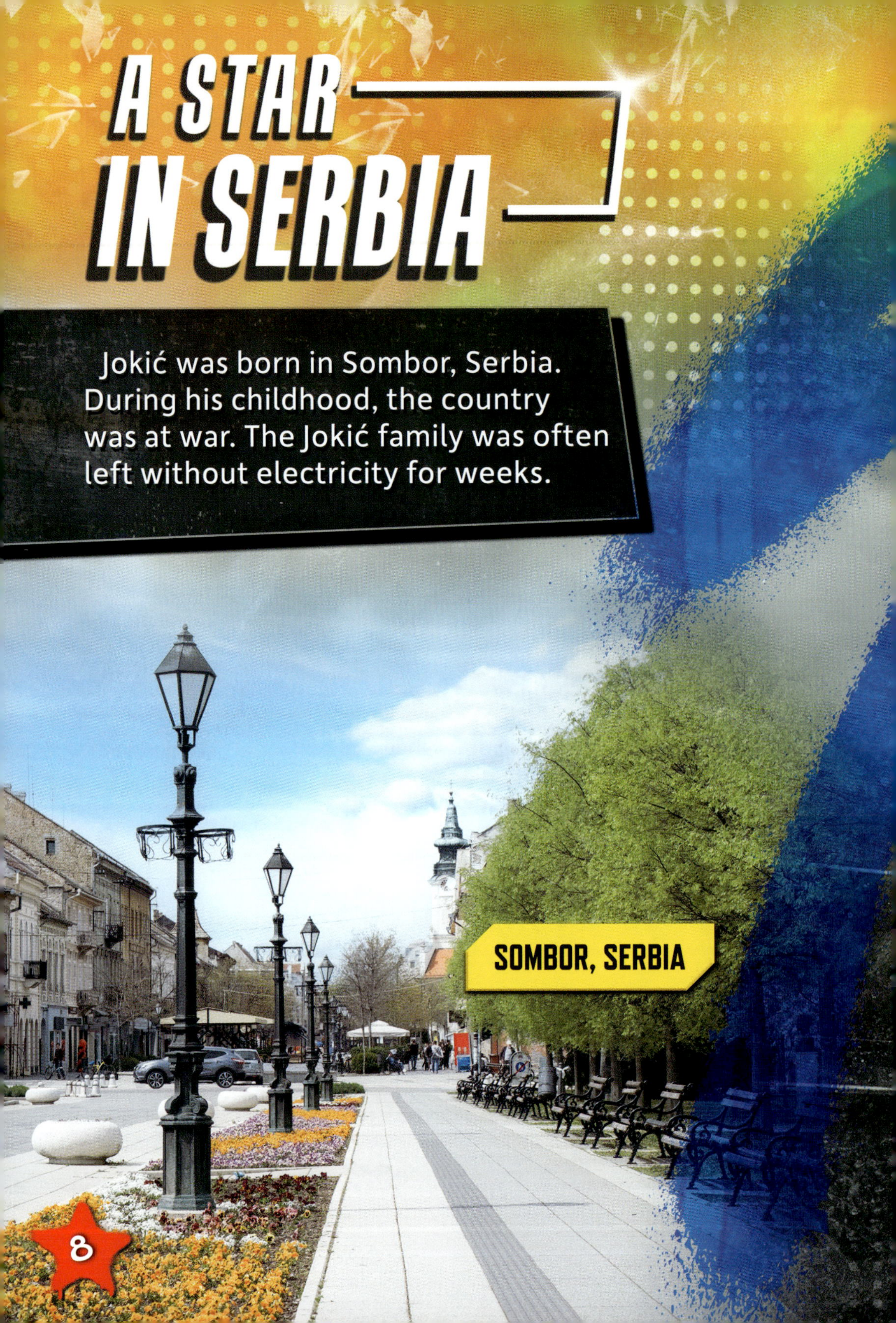

SOMBOR, SERBIA

JOKIĆ'S BROTHERS

Jokić learned basketball from his two older brothers. They played with a toy hoop in their small apartment. As Jokić grew, he quickly became skilled at passing.

Jokić joined a **professional** basketball team at age 17. He played for KK Mega Basket's junior team in Belgrade, Serbia. The next year, he joined the senior team. The Nuggets **drafted** him in 2014.

Jokić played one more year for KK Mega Basket. He was named MVP that season. He joined the Nuggets for the 2015–2016 season.

KK MEGA BASKET'S STADIUM

FAVORITES

MEAL	MOVIE	TV SHOW	SPORT OTHER THAN BASKETBALL

fish stew	*Gladiator*	*Friends*	horse racing

BECOMING AN NBA STAR

2016 SUMMER OLYMPICS

In Jokić's **rookie** season, the Nuggets did not have much success. But Jokić was named to the All-Rookie First Team in 2016. He also helped Serbia win a silver medal in the 2016 **Summer Olympics**.

Jokić kept improving. In 2017–2018, he helped the Nuggets to their first winning season in five seasons.

In the 2018–2019 season, Jokić played in his first **All-Star Game**. He helped the Nuggets reach the **playoffs**. He averaged 20.1 points per game. He also grabbed 10.8 **rebounds** per game.

Jokić played for Serbia once again in the 2019 **FIBA World Cup**. He helped the team finish in fifth place.

- KK Mega Basket, Belgrade, Serbia — 2012 to 2015
- Denver Nuggets, Denver, Colorado — 2015 to present

2019 FIBA WORLD CUP

Sombor Shuffle

Jokić has a famous move called the Sombor Shuffle. He jumps with one leg and gently tosses the ball toward the hoop.

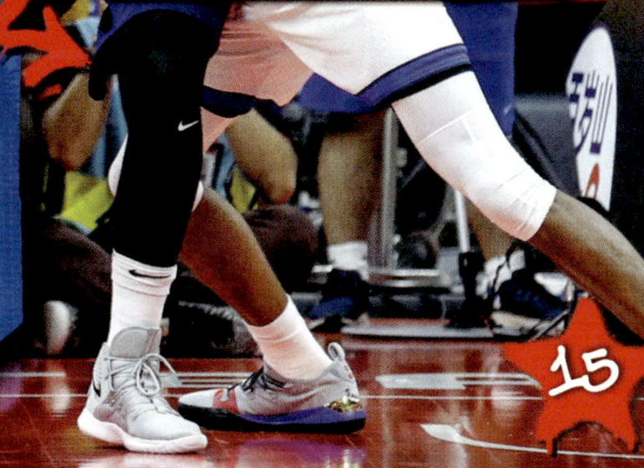

In the 2019–2020 season, Jokić led the Nuggets on a deep playoff run. They did not make it to the Finals. But Jokić was named to another All-Star Game.

Jokić won the NBA MVP award in the 2020–2021 season. The next season, he won his second straight MVP award. But the Nuggets could not advance in the playoffs.

2021 NBA MVP
TROPHY SHELF
NBA champion
2-time
NBA MVP
Finals MVP
2015–2016 NBA
All-Rookie First Team
6-time NBA All-Star

In 2023, Jokić played in his fifth All-Star Game. The Nuggets also reached the NBA Finals. Jokić helped the Nuggets win! He averaged 30.2 points, 14.0 rebounds, and 7.2 **assists** per game in the Finals.

Jokić was the first player to have a 30-point, 20-rebound, 10-assist game in the NBA Finals. He was named the Finals MVP!

2023 ALL-STAR GAME

TIMELINE

— 2012 —
Jokić joins KK Mega Basket in Serbia

— 2014 —
Jokić is drafted by the Nuggets

2023 NBA FINALS

— 2019 —

Jokić plays in his first All-Star Game

— 2022 —

Jokić wins his second straight NBA MVP

— 2023 —

The Nuggets win the NBA Finals

JOKIĆ'S FUTURE

Jokić supports a **charity** called LuBird's Light in Colorado. It raises money for playgrounds for kids of all needs.

During the offseason, Jokić trains horses in Sombor. He loves to watch them race. He wants to keep training horses when he is done playing basketball. But before then, he hopes to win more championships with the Nuggets!

GLOSSARY

All-Star Game—a game between the best players in a league

assists—passes to a teammate that result in a score

center—a player in basketball who often blocks shots and gets rebounds

championship—a contest to decide the best team or person

charity—an organization that helps others in need

drafted—chose by a process where professional teams choose high school and college athletes to play for them

FIBA World Cup—an international basketball competition held every four years

Finals—the championship series of the National Basketball Association

Most Valuable Player—the best player in a year, game, or series; the most valuable player is often called the MVP.

National Basketball Association—a professional basketball league in the United States; the National Basketball Association is often called the NBA.

playoffs—games played after the regular season is over; playoff games determine which teams play in the championship game.

professional—related to a player or team that makes money playing a sport

rebounds—when players take control of the basketball after missed shots

rookie—related to a first-year player in a sports league

Summer Olympics—a worldwide summer sports contest held in a different country every four years

TO LEARN MORE

AT THE LIBRARY

Lowe, Alexander. *G.O.A.T. Basketball Centers.* Minneapolis, Minn.: Lerner Publications, 2023.

Stabler, David. *Meet Nikola Jokić: Denver Nuggets Superstar.* Minneapolis, Minn.: Lerner Publications, 2024.

Whiting, Jim. *The Story of the Denver Nuggets.* Mankato, Minn.: Creative Education, 2023.

ON THE WEB

FACTSURFER

Factsurfer.com gives you a safe, fun way to find more information.

1. Go to www.factsurfer.com
2. Enter "Nikola Jokić" into the search box and click 🔍.
3. Select your book cover to see a list of related content.

INDEX

The images in this book are reproduced through the courtesy of: David Zalubowski/ AP Images, front cover, pp. 3, 6, 11 (Nikola Jokić), 13, 16, 20, 23; Jack Dempsey/ AP Images, pp. 4, 4-5, 18-19; Fifg/ Alamy, p. 7 (Denver Nuggets logo); Nick Wass, p. 7 (Nikola Jokić); Veronika Kovalenko, pp. 8, 11 (fish stew); AAron Ontiveroz/ Contributor/ Getty, p. 9; Banekozic/ Wikipedia, pp. 10, 15 (KK Mega Basket stadium); Collection Christophel/ Alamy, p. 11 (*Gladiator*); Album/ Alamy, p. 11 (*Friends*); dikkenss, p. 11 (horse racing); Eric Gay/ AP Images, pp. 12, 14; Jeff Zehnder/ Alamy, p. 15 (Denver Nuggets stadium); Imaginechina Limited/ Alamy, p. 15 (2019 FIBA World Cup); Dustin Bradford/ Stringer/ Getty, p. 17; Tim Nwachukwu/ Staff/ Getty, p. 18 (2023 All-Star Game); KK Mega Basket/ Wikipedia, p. 18 (KK Mega Basket logo); Denver Nuggets/ Wikipedia, p. 18 (Denver Nuggets logo); Jeff Chiu/ AP Images, p. 19 (2022); Srdjan Sevanovic/ Contributor/ Getty, p. 21.